PAUL CARTLEDGE

~

FOREVER YOUNG: WHY CAMBRIDGE HAS A PROFESSOR OF GREEK CULTURE

~

An A. G. Leventis Inaugural Lecture given in the
University of Cambridge
16 February 2009

Shaftesbury Road, Cambridge CB2 8EA, United Kingdom

One Liberty Plaza, 20th Floor, New York, NY 10006, USA

477 Williamstown Road, Port Melbourne, VIC 3207, Australia

314–321, 3rd Floor, Plot 3, Splendor Forum, Jasola District Centre, New Delhi – 110025, India

103 Penang Road, #05–06/07, Visioncrest Commercial, Singapore 238467

Cambridge University Press is part of Cambridge University Press & Assessment, a department of the University of Cambridge.

We share the University's mission to contribute to society through the pursuit of education, learning and research at the highest international levels of excellence.

www.cambridge.org
Information on this title: www.cambridge.org/9780521121729

© Paul Cartledge 2009

This publication is in copyright. Subject to statutory exception and to the provisions of relevant collective licensing agreements, no reproduction of any part may take place without the written permission of Cambridge University Press & Assessment.

First published 2009

A catalogue record for this publication is available from the British Library

ISBN 978-0-521-12172-9 Paperback

Cambridge University Press & Assessment has no responsibility for the persistence or accuracy of URLs for external or third-party internet websites referred to in this publication and does not guarantee that any content on such websites is, or will remain, accurate or appropriate.

FOREVER YOUNG: WHY CAMBRIDGE HAS A PROFESSOR OF GREEK CULTURE

The text of this inaugural lecture, delivered in the University of Cambridge on 16 February 2009, proposes that the newly established A. G. Leventis Professorship of Greek Culture is a new kind of chair: a chair not only for research but also for outreach, for the advancement of the public understanding of ancient Greek (pre-Byzantine) culture.

After explaining the Chair's origins and causes, and pondering the possible meanings of the Professorship's title, it seeks to explore and explode four 'myths' about the ancient Greeks and their culture (or cultures), myths deliberately chosen to illustrate the huge and diverse range of the Hellenic tradition that is still actively at work in our own contemporary culture. The four, in order of discussion, not necessarily of importance, are: (i) that there was an entity called 'Ancient Greece'; (ii) that the ancient Greeks were technologically backward; (iii) that the ancient Greeks really were (or looked) anything like they are depicted in such Hollywood movies as *300*; and (iv) that the Greeks invented democracy in anything like the form and sense in which we understand that institution today.

PAUL CARTLEDGE is the inaugural A. G. Leventis Professor of Greek Culture in the University of Cambridge. His many publications include *The Cambridge Illustrated History of Ancient Greece* (1997, rev. 2002), *The Greeks. A Portrait of Self and Others* (2002), *Ancient Greek Political Thought in Practice* (2009), and *Ancient Greece. A History in Eleven Cities* (2009). He holds the Gold Cross of the Order of Honour (Greece) and is an Honorary Citizen of Sparti, Greece.

To the memory of Constantinos Leventis (1938–2002)

May you always do for others
and let others do for you
                    [from Bob Dylan, 'Forever Young', 1974]

FOREVER YOUNG: WHY CAMBRIDGE HAS A PROFESSOR OF GREEK CULTURE

An A. G. Leventis Inaugural Lecture given by
Professor Paul Cartledge in the
University of Cambridge
16 February 2009

∽

Introduction

It is a very great pleasure, and a huge honour, for me to deliver this Inaugural Lecture as the first 'A. G. Leventis Professor of Greek Culture'. My thanks for facilitating this bold and innovative appointment must go, especially, to the A. G. Leventis Foundation, on the one hand, and to the Cambridge University Development Office, on the other, as well as to the Faculty of Classics and especially its Officers past and present. I thank all concerned very warmly indeed, as I thank all of you for taking the time off from doing other better things in order to be here this February evening.

I tried to pick as auspicious a time of year as possible: just four days after Charles Darwin's 200th birthday, two days after St Valentine's Day, and one day after the Lupercalia.[1] But one can never be quite certain about astral and other heavenly conjunctions – or at least I cannot, despite what I have been trying to learn about astronomical and calendrical prediction, both ancient Greek and much more recent, as we shall see. At any rate, it is crystal clear that the A. G. Leventis Foundation, whose name my chair bears, was born under a lucky star. It was founded in 1979, and named in honour of Anastasios G. Leventis (d. 1978). Originating in Cyprus, it now enjoys virtually worldwide links, with especial connections to West Africa, to the pale of Hellenic settlement ancient and modern ('Hellas' in the broad sense), and, happily, to this University. This is thanks not least to the late Constantinos ('Dino') Leventis, who matriculated at Clare College in 1956, and read Classics, and to whose memory this Inaugural Lecture is dedicated.[2] He would, I am confident, have been as delighted as we in the Classics Faculty all are to know that the Foundation's immense beneficence was playing such a key role in Cambridge's 800th campaign and in the promotion of the Arts and Humanities side of our operation. For, difficult as all fundraising is, especially in these straitened times, it is particularly so on the Arts and Humanities front.[3]

There are many advantages and blessings in being the first postholder of a chair. Not the least of them is that one does not have to be scrupulous to namecheck all one's predecessors. The downside, though, if it is a downside, is that one cannot just fall back on the tried and tested inaugural formula of revisiting an old scholarly battleground, lining up and duly praising or burying one's allies and foes, and then retiring behind the parapet, as if the battle – or skirmish – had never occurred. Instead, as an Inaugural professor, exposed and without much cover, one has to be very careful indeed how one surveys the scene and marks out one's terrain – or territory. For the Leventis Chair of Greek Culture is in my conception not just a new chair (the first to be endowed within the Classics Faculty at Cambridge since World War II), but also and more importantly a new *kind* of chair – in ancient Greek terms, a *kathedra* that is not just *nea*, but *kainê* or even *kainotomos*. Hence, the bulk of this particular Inaugural Lecture – not entirely unlike a certain other Inaugural delivered in Washington, DC, last month – will be about the Chair's meaning and purposes, as I see or envision them.[4]

Culture and causation

I begin with a seeming paradox. There have been Professors of Culture or Cultural History before, including in this University, but to my knowledge there is only one other Professor of Ancient Greek Culture anywhere else in the world.[5] Yet all but one word of my title are not Greek in etymology, but Latin, even though so much else of our English vocabulary (gigabyte, terabyte...) *is* Greek-derived.[6] But such was the cultural and ideological as well as military and political power of the ancient Romans and their Latin language that typically we speak of ancient 'Greece' and 'Greeks', not 'Hellas' or 'Hellenes' (which is what they called themselves then and call themselves today). In fact, the only non-Latinate word of my title is 'Leventis': Greek, though borrowed from Ottoman Turkish. But thereby hangs a tale, a suitably punning one, as I would not want to disappoint those of you who know of my fatal addiction to paronomasia: for 'Leventis' connotes youth.[7]

The second half of my lecture title, 'Why Cambridge Has a Professor of Greek Culture', is rather more obvious etymologically, but perhaps a bit more complicated conceptually and semantically. It is borrowed from and modelled on a very different kind of work of art: not a pop song, but a general-interest academic volume aimed at a wide audience: *Why Humans Have Cultures*, by Michael Carrithers (1992). Carrithers, suitably enough, is an anthropologist (a good Greek-derived word), and his book is explicitly about 'anthropology and social diversity'. Which, in a way, is exactly what this lecture, and my title, are also all about, in a comparativist – ancient/modern, ancient Greek/contemporary world – cultural perspective or conceptual framework.

The 'Why' of my subtitle can be read either retrospectively (= 'how come?') or prospectively (= 'what for?').[8] Modern Greek, not always the richest of languages, in this case gets that distinction rather nicely, using three words that together capture the salient nuances of our English 'why': *aphou* = from what (origin)?, *dioti* = on account of what?, *giati* = for what purpose(s)? The short answer to the retrospective 'why' is the exceptional, indeed phenomenal generosity of the A. G. Leventis Foundation. This is not the place, and there is not the time, to do anything like justice to the reach and the penetration of the Foundation's beneficence and benefactions: perhaps I could just say that in this University there is in the Fitzwilliam Museum an A. G. Leventis Gallery of Cypriot Antiquities and at Clare College a Leventis Graduate Scholarship in pre-Byzantine Hellenic studies; that elsewhere in this country the Hellenic Society distributes grants for various purposes to secondary schools of all kinds owing to the generosity of the Leventis Foundation; and that abroad the Foundation's scholarly and civic interests extend as far and as variously afield as the long-established Metropolitan Museum in New York and the recently revived Archaeological Museum of Odessa in the Ukraine.[9] The answer to the prospective sense of 'why' in my title constitutes most of the rest of the lecture.

First, let me make some attempt to pin down the butterfly word 'culture', a protean term of many possible meanings. I start with what might properly be called its 'anthropological' sense, as used non-judgmentally by Carrithers.[10] By this is meant a society's regime or social regimen, a way of life, taken as a whole – although I am only too well aware that there can be cultures within a culture, not least in the case of ancient Greece.[11] But 'culture' may also be used, or taken, in a broadly aesthetic sense as equivalent to 'civilisation', which can soon acquire an evaluative, or judgmental, connotation as meaning civilisation (or a civilisation) as opposed to barbarism, or as high (versus low) culture, or elite (versus popular, mass) culture.[12] The modern Greek word for 'culture' in this evaluative sense – as in The Foundation for Hellenic Culture – is *politismos*, which is a word adopted into modern Greek, not through Latin or Ottoman Turkish, but by attraction from the ancient Greek word *polis* (the root of our 'politics', etc.) and its implication, following Aristotle, that citification was civilisation.[13] The all-conquering sub-branch of History labelled 'cultural history' – there is an International Society for Cultural History and in this University, for instance, a Modern Cultural History Seminar – can usefully embrace any one or all of these various and contested meanings.[14]

Myths

Rather than prolong the etymologising or definition-grinding, let me try to explain, using examples from my own and others' research, what sorts of cultural artefacts I think a (any) Leventis Professor could or even should be concerned to analyse, explain and promote. I shall do so using the good old English (Greek-derived) word 'myth', not in any academic sense but in its popular or vulgar sense of something believed to be true, but in fact more or less false. In Aristotelian vein[15] I shall give four examples, the common theme of which is difference: for although the ancient Greeks (or some of them) are in many fundamental ways key cultural ancestors of us in the 'West' today, their culture(s) was/were often very different in no less fundamental ways.[16]

Myth 1. That there really ever was an entity properly called 'Ancient Greece'.

In fact, during the period usually understood to be covered by that phrase – say from 1500 BC(E) to the conquest of Greece by Rome (in the mid second century BCE) – there were lots of often very dissimilar Greek communities/cities, about 1,000 at any one time, scattered from one end of the Mediterranean and Black Seas to the other; they usually were radically self-differentiated, and typically thought of themselves as, say, 'Athenians' or 'Spartans' first, and 'Greeks' (or rather 'Hellenes') quite a long way second.[17] In a little book that is forthcoming this autumn, entitled *Ancient Greece*, I have selected just eleven out of the 1,000 or so, precisely in order to illustrate just how diverse 'Ancient Greece' really was.[18] I begin with Cnossus in Crete, because that is where the earliest texts in the ancient Greek language have been found – though we learned that only in 1952, when the script unromantically labelled 'Linear B' was finally deciphered as recording the earliest known form of Greek by architect Michael Ventris, aided indispensably by Cambridge philologist John Chadwick.[19] I first heard Chadwick lecture on the subject when I was a schoolboy, because he happened to have gone to the same school as I (St Paul's in London, a mere 500 years old this year), but I first met him properly when I came to Cambridge in 1979 and he was exceedingly kind and helpful to me as a struggling 'metic' (resident alien). It therefore gives me especial pleasure that the New Greek on-line Lexicon currently being prepared in the Cambridge Classics Faculty is both inspired by him and funded by, among other principal donors, the Leventis Foundation.[20]

I end my little history of Ancient Greece with the city of Byzantion, founded in the Golden Horn sometime early in the seventh century BCE, which in 324 CE became

Constantinople and in 1453 Istanbul (the name possibly derived from a good ancient as well as modern Greek phrase meaning 'to or at the City'). Within that one geographical frame are encapsulated in miniature many of the most interesting aspects of the characteristically urban experience of the ancient – and not so ancient – Hellenes.[21] But I devote chapters also to among others Athens, Thebes, Alexandria and Sparta, bringing out what I take to be their most salient contributions to the remarkable cultural amalgam that was – or rather is now seen as – Ancient Greece.

Myth 2. That the ancient Greeks were utterly technologically backward.

The burden of this claim – or accusation – is that, although they or some of them were outstandingly brilliant in theory (Greek word), and especially in the field of mathematics (ditto), they had little or no notion of practical applied technology (ditto). Now, by comparison to us, they were indeed backward in all sorts of ways – to call a spade a spade. Indeed, to continue the horticultural motif, they may not even have had a word for a wheelbarrow... [22] However, recent truly scientific research – the international Antikythera Mechanism Research Project, which uses the latest technology including an X-ray machine weighing 8 tons specially designed to deliver 3-D X-ray computed tomography (CT) – has transformed our understanding of one particular piece of ancient Greek technology, and maybe also of ancient Greek mentality and culture too. The 'Antikythera Mechanism' is so called because that is where it was serendipitously found, by a team of temporarily marooned Greek sponge-divers in 1900, in a wreck lying off a small islet between the southern Greek mainland and northwest Crete. I first heard of the object during the early 1970s, when I was researching an archaeological doctoral thesis that took the whole of Laconia and its offshore islands for its geographical province.[23] Few others had heard of it then. Today, the Mechanism is famous enough to justify the publication of articles in the leading science journal, *Nature*, and an exhibition and one-day conference held at Cambridge's Whipple Museum of the History of Science.[24]

Scholarship remains divided over the Mechanism's ultimate purpose and function: was it a proto-clockwork mechanism, or might it justly even be dignified by the title of 'proto-computer'?[25] At any rate, the Mechanism, crafted probably in around 100 BCE, in what we call the Hellenistic period of ancient Greek history, was unquestionably devised for making astronomical calculations and predictions of an extremely sophisticated kind, further developing sightings and insights achieved hundreds of years before by Babylonians. The name of Archimedes has been mooted, over-optimistically perhaps, as a possible godfather on the theoretical side behind some of the maths involved, but even he – who had been killed in 212 BCE, a century or more before the Mechanism was made – would I suspect have been astonished by the intricate craft-skill, the *tekhnê*, that went into its making. Nothing remotely like it – more than thirty bronze gear-wheels, precisely cut, accompanied by various scales, pointers and inscriptions – had been known from Antiquity, and nothing remotely like it was to be known again, anywhere, for at least a further millennium, if not until the Renaissance. How hugely more ignorant we would have been of the ancient Greeks' potential for applied theory but for this huge accident of discovery, is a sobering as well as a stimulating thought. A thought entirely suitable, I suggest, for this International Year of Astronomy.

Myth 3. That the ancient Greeks were (or looked) anything much like they are represented in Hollywood movies.
From the real, celestial stars I pass to the Tinseltown versions. From high culture, elite culture indeed, I now shift gears – downwards? – to an example drawn from the massiest of mass or popular culture. I shall focus on the Hollywood film *300* (2007), for which I was a bit-part

academic consultant,[26] because I want to bring out not merely how wrong, historically, but also, and much more importantly, just how – potentially – dangerous as well as entertaining and provocative in the best sense these ancient-world movies can be. That is, despite being terribly wrong in terms of historical fact, such movies can nevertheless excite a genuine and ultimately even scholarly passion for studying the ancient Greeks, and in this case the ancient Spartans. But they can also pander to, even inflame, the worst kind of cultural contempt, and indeed hatreds.

I must preface my necessarily laconic remarks by saying that 'reception-studies' – studying what traces the ancient Greeks have left and continue to leave on our contemporary culture – is currently a very hot subject-area for scholarship.[27] This applies not just to movies, of course, but also to historical novels, video games and even iPhone 3-D action games. There is a very widespread thirst among a large public for genuine knowledge about ancient Sparta. I have lost count of the number of email solicitations I have received for help with high-school or undergraduate tests; I have had official requests for my books from US Marines officials, and I am slightly awestruck that British soldiers have gone into battle in Afghanistan tattooed with slogans inspired by their profound respect for the heroic deeds of Spartan

King Leonidas and his 300 men at Thermopylae in 480 BCE.[28]

Which brings me back to the movie *300*'s first (and by no means last) historical mistake – its very title. Even if we count only the Spartans present at the Hot Gates, there were unquestionably 301 of them – 300 *plus* Leonidas; and that is without counting the non-Spartan Laconians (known as Perioeci), and the other loyalist Greek allies, especially those of Thespiae who died to a man, making a total force of some 6–7,000. The movie, like its direct source, a graphic novel, is deafeningly silent about them. Nor did Spartans in 480 BCE – or at any other time – go into battle wearing little more body-protection than spandex briefs, however much they may have celebrated the typically Hellenic cultural devotion to the nude male body off the battlefield. Nor did they go on campaign or into battle unsupported: Sparta, like most of the other 1,000 or so Greek cities, was a society based on slavery, and members of the Spartans' serf-like servile underclass, who were themselves Greeks, were also crucially present at Thermopylae.[29]

To be fair, though, the movie does not get everything factually wrong about the Spartans: it is right to highlight the quite un-Hellenic public role of a Spartan wife and mother, admittedly an exceptional woman, Queen Gorgo; and it captures well the Spartans' calculated, fight-to-the-death attitude to life as expressed in a number of quintessentially and authentically laconic one-liners. But – and it is a huge 'but' – the movie gets just about everything possible historically wrong about the Spartans' opponents, the Persian Empire and its subjects. And especially about the Persians themselves, from the top down. Whatever the real Great King Xerxes may have been, he was not a multiply pierced and hypertrophied drag-Queen-style God-Monarch. I therefore had every sympathy with the Iranian delegation to the United Nations when it issued a public protest against this cultural denigration of their – as they chose to see them – ancestors. On the other hand, I am quite sure the Iranians were wrong in seeing the movie as a quasi-official, politically calculated weapon in the Bush Administration's clash-of-civilisations War on Terror. Nevertheless, their response and its echoes among the wider public are an object lesson in the fact that such movies can never be 'merely' or 'purely' figments of entertainment.[30]

Myth 4. That the Greeks invented 'democracy' in anything like the form and sense that we give to that word and institution today.

Here I shall use as my final example or test-case the trial and death of Socrates in 399 BCE, condemned on charges of impiety and political subversion.[31]

Contrary to most scholars, I argue that Socrates was found guilty mainly on grounds of his alleged impiety, since in Ancient Greece religion was thoroughly politicised, and not chiefly because of his alleged political subversion; and – even more controversially – that his 501 Athenian judges, mostly ordinary Athenians, were right, according to the lights of their own democratic culture, both to find him guilty and to condemn him to death. Actually, Socrates need not have died even so – if he was a martyr (Greek word) to freedom of thought and speech, he was in the fullest sense a voluntary martyr. But what matters in the present context is, as Louis Macneice once put it, how 'unimaginably different' it all was there and then.[32] Whatever the original ancient Greek – Athenian – democracy may actually have been, and however we might want to characterise it today, it emphatically was not a modern-style, liberal, representative, Western democracy. Not that that makes it any the less interesting or important to study, from a comparativist, cultural-historical point of view. On the contrary: as a well-known novel begins, 'The past is a foreign country: they do things differently there.'[33] And usually one does learn more from comparisons that bring out and highlight key differences than from those that merely elicit or emphasise possibly deceptive or superficial similarities.

Usually – not invariably: for I should like in closing to venture a transcultural, philosophical constant, drawing, for the purpose, upon an ancient Greek historian, possibly the original 'Historian' properly so called, who is very close to my heart as well as my head. Herodotus of Halicarnassus was born *c.* 484 BCE, and his *Histories* of the Graeco-Persian Wars of 480–479 and their antecedents were somehow 'published' during the 430s and 420s in the shadow of the Graeco-Greek Peloponnesian War between Sparta and Athens and their respective allies (431–404 BCE). Herodotus, as Edward Gibbon perceptively observed, 'sometimes writes for children, and sometimes for philosophers', i.e., both tells rattling good yarns and (yet also) has something valuable to say to enlightened people of the world who believe – perhaps naively – that it is both desirable and possible to learn from history.[34] Here I want to cite a characteristically philosophical notion which Herodotus typically places in the mouth of a wise, or at least wised-up, barbarian (non-Greek) potentate. The notion is the perhaps rather pessimistic one of a perpetual cycle in human fortunes:

> My suffering, though joyless for me, has taught me many lessons ... If you [Cyrus] realize that you are human ... consider first that there is a cycle in human affairs, and as it goes around it does not permit the same person to enjoy good fortune for ever.[35]

So the once fabulously wealthy *ex*-King Croesus of Lydia rather ruefully observes to his new overlord, Emperor Cyrus of Persia. And so we might want to observe today to certain once mighty but now fallen investment-banker lords of the universe. But what goes down may also come up. In the 1980s, not long after I had joined Clare College as a teaching Fellow and Director of Studies in Classics, one of my many brilliant and congenial undergraduate students was among the very first to be wooed to the City of London after her graduation with a 'golden hello'. That was then: a world of the 'Big Bang' and big red braces (at least for the boys). Today, however, in these very different, dismally credit-crunched times, I am happy to be able to recommend to my brightest and best students a rather more steady and surely more deeply fulfilling job, or profession, one with prospects – in Academia.

Or, looking even further forward, as far forward indeed as is possible in this life on earth, let me quote what one of Herodotus' Greek characters, wiseacre Solon of Athens, sagely recommends to the aforementioned oriental plutocrat Croesus, then still in his pomp: 'look to the end' – the end in the sense both of terminus and of goal.[36] For it is, he argues, in light of that end, and only in that light, that it will be known finally whether one has not just lived but lived well. Living well, the state or condition of *eudaimonia*, was the final aim of the very best reflection produced by the greatest examplars of ancient Greek culture, figures such as perhaps the master of them all, Aristotle, whose name, accidentally but not incidentally, means just that: 'best end' (*ariston telos*).

To conclude: if my maths are right, I have in this lecture used some fifty words of ancient Greek derivation – a sure sign, if a small one, of the indebtedness of our contemporary culture to that of the ancient Greeks. I have done so in pursuit of my overriding aim of trying to justify a fresh vision of the new Leventis Chair. For I envision it not only as a research chair but also as an outreach chair, for the Advancement of the Public Understanding of Ancient Greek Culture, perhaps;[37] and, as such, as a vital part of this University's determined efforts to maximise access to, and the distribution of, the benefits to be derived from the pursuit of our collective goal of 'transforming tomorrow'.[38]

NOTES

1 For St Valentine's and the Lupercalia, see Blackburn and Holford-Strevens 2000, s.vv.
2 Dino was followed to Clare, though not alas to the Classics Faculty, in 1960 by his younger brother Charalambos 'Harry' Leventis, now a Trustee of the A. G. Leventis Foundation together with his surviving brother Anastasios 'Tasos' P. Leventis, the Foundation's chairman.
3 I agree entirely with the Vice-Chancellor, Professor Alison Richard, that 'The key challenge [of the 800th Anniversary Campaign] is raising funds': interview of the Vice-Chancellor with *The Cambridge Student*, 22 January 2009, p. 17. I sat on the '800th Committee', formally the University's Joint Committee on Development chaired by the Vice-Chancellor, from its inception to the end of 2008. On the Humanities and fundraising, see further below, n. 14.
4 The current US President's Inaugural may conveniently be read in Obama 2009, which contains also Abraham Lincoln's First and Second Presidential Inaugural Addresses (1861, 1865), his Gettysburg Address (1863), and Ralph Waldo Emerson's 'Self-Reliance' (1841).

5 Phillip Mitsis is Alexander S. Onassis Professor of Hellenic Culture and Civilisation at New York University, principally in the Faculty of Classics, where since 2006 I have held the (visiting) Hellenic Parliament Global Distinguished Professorship in the Theory and History of Democracy.

6 For Latin and English, see Janson 2004: 172–4. In July 2009, I delivered to the University's International Summer School a plenary lecture on the subject of 'Understanding English, via Greek': how could we get by without, for instance, 'spartan' (below, n. 29) or the marvellously onomatopoeic 'borborygmus' (below, n. 20)? After the lecture, Professor John Parker, Director of Cambridge's Botanic Garden, kindly wrote to me: 'From the days of my D.Phil. (Latin) at Oxford, I have been studying and teaching about CHROMOSOMES, trying to get students to understand the process of MEIOSIS, to talk about CHIASMATA and their significance, at the stage of PACHYNEMA, and occasionally straying to the strandedness of POLYTENY – and so on. Oh how I enjoyed my few years of Greek after the stultification of Latin and what joy to land in a research world of terminology of such interesting etymology.' On a somewhat less elevated plane perhaps, I can strongly recommend both Fiada 2003 and, even funnier, Higgins 2008.

7 Defined, according to the *Redhouse Turkish/Ottoman–English Dictionary* (1997), as 'a handsome, strong youth', something like the Greek *pallêkari*; cf. 'fine upstanding fellow; brave or generous man', by *The Oxford Dictionary of Modern Greek*, compiled by J. T. Pring (Oxford, 1982); the quality of *leventeia*, according to Patrick Leigh Fermor 2003: 103–4, 'embraces a range of characteristics', the first of which is listed as 'youth'. That in turn accounts for my lecture title 'Forever Young', itself borrowed – as the 'bobcats' will

instantly have recognised – from the title of a rather apt 1974 Bob Dylan song. ('Forever Young' was also used as the title for a 1992 Hollywood movie, a reworking of a kind of fable at least as old as Aristotle's day, in which people who fall asleep in one era wake up in another, such as the pre-Christian/early-Christian Seven Sleepers of Ephesus: www.newadvent.org/cathen/05496a.htm)

8 On the 'problem' of causation – especially the issues of 'too many causes' and so of deciding 'what made the difference' – see Hart and Honoré 1985; Beebee *et al.* 2009.

9 Karageorghis, Vassilika and Wilson 1999; Brehme *et al.* 2001; Karageorghis 2005.

10 Carrithers 1992; perhaps, in light of the current stand-off within the discipline of anthropology (Fearn 2008) one should emphasise that Carrithers practises social, not evolutionary, anthropology. See further Haddon 1934; Geertz 1983; Carrithers *et al.* 1985; Finley 1986; Okeley 1996; Olwig and Hastrup 1996; Kuper 2001; Sahlins 2001; Wagner 1981; and above all Lukes 2008, which I read only after delivering the lecture. Lukes traces the concept of moral relativism back to Herodotus, but I should say rather that he was a pluralist, although he has also been read as an absolutist!

11 Dougherty and Kurke 2003: as their collection's subtitle has it, contact, collaboration, but also (a great deal of) conflict.

12 As Scruton 2007 puts it, 'culture counts'; or, as the movie director Fritz Lang, playing himself in J.-L. Godard's *Le mépris* of 1963, remarked (quoted in Pomeroy 2008, 81 and n. 51): 'Whenever I hear the word culture, I bring out my checkbook'. On the other hand, as Edward Pearce has observed (*New Statesman*, 9 March 2009), it can also be seen as 'something superior to be resented'. See further Cartwright 1993; Eagleton 1999; Dix 2008.

13 Babiniotis 2000. On 'Ancient Greece' as a culture or civilisation of cities, see Cartledge 2009a.
14 'Cultural history' has of late captured the castle of History, taking over the mantle of 'social history': Cartledge 2002; Burke 2008; cf. Osborne 2007; and the current, 2008–10, research topic of the Shelby Cullom Davis Center for Historical Studies at Princeton, 'Cultures and Institutions in Motion'. Beard 2008, 117 rightly observes that the Humanities definitionally address 'the central issues that face humanity: questions of cultural and religious difference, of contested definitions of culture, propriety, art, freedom, or good governance'. Note also Osborne 2008, 6: 'The challenge is to make sure that we [Humanities subjects] matter not simply because we cost money, but because what we do makes a difference... we should be measured by the transformation we effect in the... whole lives of those who hear and read us'.
15 Aristotle was a stickler for precise taxonomy, at least in theory. For example, in the *Politics* he identified four species each of the genera of *politeia* (constitution) that usually were just broadly labelled either *oligarkhia* (rule of a few) or *dêmokratia* (power of the Dêmos, either the citizen People as a whole or the poor majority of them, the masses).
16 Other 'myths' that I could have addressed here – on all of which I have written, spoken or debated – include: 'Black Athena'; cultural property – especially the Parthenon; the Olympics (and the Olympic Truce Movement); and Alexander the Great and the name of 'Macedonia'.
17 Cartledge ed. 1997; Hansen and Nielsen 2004.
18 Cartledge 2009a.
19 Chadwick 1967.
20 I understand that, sadly, there is to be no entry for that marvellously onomatopoeic word 'borborygmus' – see the latest,

eleventh, edition of *The Concise Oxford Dictionary* (2004, rev. 2006), s.v.; but that is because the Hippocratic Corpus of medical writings is, for reasons of space and specialised vocabulary, not to be counted among the New Lexicon's source-texts.

21 See above, n. 13. But in fairness I should also cite Vlassopoulos 2007, a salutary counterblast by a former pupil.

22 Not in all ways, of course: see Cuomo 2007, a volume in the 'Key Themes in Ancient History' series that I co-edit with Peter Garnsey. But I note that there is no entry for 'wheelbarrow' in Oleson ed. 2008; see, for a succinct account of 'The Greek and Roman view of technology', Oleson in Oleson ed. 2008: 3–6.

23 'Early Lakedaimon *c.* 950–650 BC. An Archaeological and Historical Study' (1975). Supervised by John (now Professor Sir John) Boardman, and examined by Martin Robertson and George Forrest.

24 Freeth *et al.* 2008, with a foreword by the Museum's director, Dr Liba Taub; cf. generally Hannah 2009: index s.v. 'Antikythera Mechanism'.

25 See Marchant 2008, a popular-science book.

26 My advisory role was confined to one long telephone conversation with the production studio in Montreal, during which I was asked to suggest pronunciations for certain ancient Greek personal and other kinds of names. Needless to add, in the case of one of the most prominent names (Leonidas), my advice was not heeded.

27 See generally Nisbet 2008; Pomeroy 2008; and Richards 2008. I have myself co-edited with F. Rose Greenland *Responses to Oliver Stone's **Alexander**. Film, History, and Cultural Studies* (Madison: University of Wisconsin Press, forthcoming).

28 I am currently in discussions with Mr 'Ultramarathon Man', the Greek-American Dean Karnazes, regarding his proposed

re-enactment of a famous run – by an Athenian, admittedly – from Athens to Sparta and back, at the time of the original (Battle of) Marathon in August or September 490 BCE. The potential connection with the impending London Olympiad of 2012 requires no emphasis.

29 The derogatory label the Spartans applied to them, 'Helot' (captive), has entered the English language, along with 'spartan' and 'laconic': Cartledge 2004. There has even been a historical novel of that title (2008).

30 Probably the best published scholarly response to *300* is Champion *et al.* 2007; but see also Nisbet 2008. For an attempt to keep the record of Thermopylae as historically straight as it can be, see Cartledge 2007. On the entertainment versus 'reality' problematic, see Daniel Mendelsohn's acute review of two '9/11' movies, in the context of a reading of Aeschylus's *Persians*: Mendelsohn 2008, 442–53 (originally 21 September 2006).

31 I have discussed this in much greater detail in Cartledge 2009b, ch. 7. See already Cartledge 2008, Lecture 3; and most recently, and more conventionally, Waterfield 2009.

32 *Autumn Journal* (1939, repr. Faber & Faber, 1996), stanza ix.

33 L. P. Hartley, *The Go-Between* (1953).

34 E. Gibbon, *The Decline and Fall of the Roman Empire*, vol. I, ch. 24, n. 52, in the 3-volume edition of D. Womersley (London: Allen Lane, 1994); cf. D. Asheri, 'General Introduction' in Asheri *et al.* 2007, 36–7: 'In a sense, H. is more of a philosopher than a historian, if "philosophy", in the Ionian sense of the word, is primarily the search for Being in Becoming'. *If* . . . As Geoffrey Lloyd (who with typical generosity and dispatch vetted a near-final draft of this published lecture) reminds me, 'philosophy' was – and is – just as problematic a concept as 'history'.

35 1.207.1–2, in the new translation by A. Purvis in Strassler 2007.

36 1.32.9. Among the many recent publications of and on Herodotus, I would single out Irwin and Greenwood eds. 2007, a Cambridge product in every sense.
37 See already Cartledge 1998a, 1998b, and 2005.
38 'Transforming Tomorrow' is one of the catchy slogans devised for the promotion of Cambridge's '800th' campaign; see above, n. 3. It is a source of special pride to be part of a winning research culture both in my Faculty of Classics and in the University as a whole. Likewise, it is an honour as well as a pleasure to acknowledge the help and support I have been afforded at the Cambridge University Press by above all Mr Stephen Bourne, Mr Richard Fisher, and Dr Michael Sharp.

REFERENCES

∼

Asheri, D., A. Lloyd, and A. Corcella (2007) *A Commentary on Herodotus Books I–IV*, ed. O. Murray and A. Moreno. Oxford University Press

Avery, R. and S. Bezmez, eds. (1997) *The Redhouse Turkish/Ottoman–English Dictionary*. Hopkins, MN

Babiniotis, G. (2000) 'To politistiko elleima tês politikês', *To Vima*, 3 September

Beard, M. (2008) 'Arts and humanities. From Sophocles to semiotics', *The University of Cambridge. An 800th Anniversary Portrait*, ed. P. Pagnamenta. London: Third Millennium, 115–17

Beebee, H., C. Hitchcock and P. Menzies, eds. (2009) *The Oxford Handbook of Causation*. Oxford University Press

Blackburn, B. and L. Holford-Strevens (2000) *The Oxford Book of Days*. Oxford University Press

Brehme, S. *et al.* (2001) *Ancient Cypriote Art in Berlin*. Nicosia: A. G. Leventis Foundation and the Staatliche Museen zu Berlin

Burke, P. (2008) *What Is Cultural History?* 2nd edn. Cambridge: Polity Press

Carrithers, M. (1992) *Why Humans Have Cultures. Explaining Anthropology and Social Diversity*. Oxford University Press

Carrithers, M., S. Collins and S. Lukes, eds. (1985) *The Category of the Person. Anthropology, Philosophy, History*. Cambridge University Press

Cartledge, P., ed. (1997) *The Cambridge Illustrated History of Ancient Greece*. Cambridge University Press [updated pb. repr. 2002]

Cartledge, P. (1998a) 'Cambridge Classics for the third millennium', *Cambridge Contributions*, ed. S. Ormrod. Cambridge University Press: 103–21

(1998b) 'Classics: from discipline in crisis to (multi)cultural capital?' in *Pedagogy and Power. Rhetorics of Classical Learning*, ed. Y. L. Too and N. Livingstone. Cambridge University Press: 16–28

(2002) 'What is social history now?' in *What Is History Now?*, ed. D. Cannadine. Basingstoke: Palgrave Macmillan: 19–35

(2004) 'What have the Spartans done for us?: Sparta's contribution to Western civilisation', *Greece & Rome*, 2nd ser., 51.2: 164–79

(2005) 'Why/how does Classics matter?' in *Arts and Humanities in Higher Education* 4.2 (June 2005), ed. S. Ormrod, 185–99

(2007) *Thermopylae. The Battle That Changed the World*, new edn. London: Pan Macmillan, New York: Vintage

(2008) *Eine Trilogie über die Demokratie*. Steiner Verlag Stuttgart

(2009a) *Ancient Greece. A History in Eleven Cities*. Oxford University Press

(2009b) *Ancient Greek Political Thought in Practice*. Cambridge University Press

Cartwright, J. (1993) 'Culture', *The Independent Magazine*, 3 July: 14–15

Chadwick, J. (1967) *The Decipherment of Linear B*, 2nd edn. Cambridge University Press [repr. 1990]

Champion, C., S. Basu and E. Lasch-Quinn (2007) '*300*: The use and abuse of history', *The Classical Outlook* 85.1 (Fall): 28–32

Cuomo, S. (2007) *Technology and Culture in Greek and Roman Antiquity*. Cambridge University Press

Dix, H. (2008) *After Raymond Williams. Cultural Materialism and the Break-up of Britain*. Cardiff: University of Wales Press

Dougherty, C. and L. Kurke eds. (2003) *The Cultures Within Ancient Greek Culture. Contact, Conflict, Collaboration*. Cambridge University Press

Eagleton, T. (1999) *The Idea of Culture*. Oxford: Blackwell

Fearn, H. (2008) 'The great divide', *Times Higher Education*, 20 November: 36–9

Fiada, A. (2003) *The Xenophobe's Guide to the Greeks*, new edn. London: Ravette Books

Finley, M. (1986) 'Anthropology and the Classics', in his *The Use and Abuse of History*, new edn. London: The Hogarth Press, 102–19

Freeth, Tony, *et al.* (2008) *The Antikythera Mechanism. Decoding an Ancient Greek Mystery*. Cambridge: Whipple Museum of the History of Science

Geertz, C. (1983) *The Interpretation of Cultures*. Glasgow: Fontana

Golden, M. and P. Toohey, eds. (1997) *Inventing Ancient Culture. Historicism, Periodization, and the Ancient World*. London and New York: Routledge

Haddon, A. C. (1934) *History of Anthropology. An Ideal Introduction to the Science of Anthropology*. London: Watts & Co.

Hannah, R. (2009) *Time in Antiquity*. Abingdon and New York: Routledge

Hansen, M. H. and T. H. Nielsen (2004) *An Inventory of Archaic and Classical Poleis*. Oxford University Press

Hart, H. L. A. and T. Honoré (1985) *Causation in the Law*, 2nd edn. Oxford: Clarendon Press [original edn, 1959]

Higgins, C. (2008) *It's All Greek to Me*. London: Short Books

Irwin, E. and E. Greenwood, eds. (2007) *Reading Herodotus. A Study of the Logoi in Book 5 of Herodotus' Histories*. Cambridge University Press

Janson, T. (2004) *A Natural History of Latin. The Story of the World's Most Successful Language*. Oxford University Press

Karageorghis, V. (2005) *Ancient Cypriote Art in Russian Museums*. Nicosia: A. G. Leventis Foundation

Karageorghis, V., E. Vassilika, and P. Wilson (1999) *The Art of Ancient Cyprus in the Fitzwilliam Museum, Cambridge*. Cambridge: The Fitzwilliam Museum and the A. G. Leventis Foundation

Kuper, A. (2001) *Culture. The Anthropologist's Account*. Cambridge, MA: Harvard University Press

Leigh Fermor, P. (2003) 'The island of leventeiá' (originally 1966), repr. in *Words of Mercury*, ed. A. Cooper. London: John Murray, 97–105

Lukes, S. (2008) *Moral Relativism*. London: Profile

Marchant, J. (2008) *Decoding the Heavens. Solving the Mystery of the World's First Computer*. London: William Heinemann

Mendelsohn, D. (2008) *How Beautiful It Is and How Easily It Can Be Broken*. New York: HarperCollins

Nisbet, G. (2008) *Ancient Greece in Film and Popular Culture*, 2nd edn. Exeter: Bristol Phoenix Press

Obama, B. (2009) *The Inaugural Address 2009. Together with Abraham Lincoln's First and Second Inaugural Addresses and The Gettysburg Address and Ralph Waldo Emerson's Self-Reliance*. London: Penguin

Okeley, J. (1996) *Own or Other Culture?* London and New York: Routledge

Oleson, J. P., ed. (2008) *The Oxford Handbook of Engineering & Technology in the Classical World*. Oxford University Press

Olwig, K. F. and K. Hastrup, eds. (1996) *Siting Culture. The Shifting Anthropological Object*. London and New York: Routledge

Osborne, R., ed. (2007) *Debating the Athenian Cultural Revolution. Art, Literature, Philosophy, and Politics, 430–380 B.C.* Cambridge and New York: Cambridge University Press

   (2008) 'Realisation', *The Oxford Magazine* (Fifth Week, Michaelmas Term) 5–6

Ostler, N. (2005) *Empires of the Word. A Language History of the World*. London: HarperCollins

Pomeroy, A. (2008) *Then It Was Destroyed by the Volcano. The Ancient World in Film and On Television*. London: Duckworth

Richards, J. (2008) *Hollywood's Ancient Worlds*. London: Continuum

Sahlins, M. (2001) *Culture in Practice. Selected Essays*. New York: Zone Books

Scruton, R. (2007) *Culture Counts*. London: Encounter Books

Strassler, R., ed. (2007) *The Landmark Herodotus*. New York: Pantheon Books

Vlassopoulos, K. (2007) *Unthinking the Greek Polis. Ancient Greek History Beyond Eurocentrism*. Cambridge University Press

Wagner, R. (1981) *The Invention of Culture*, rev. and expanded edn. University of Chicago Press

Waterfield, R. (2009) *Why Socrates Died. Dispelling the Myths*. London: Faber and Faber

For EU product safety concerns, contact us at Calle de José Abascal, 56-1°,
28003 Madrid, Spain or eugpsr@cambridge.org.

www.ingramcontent.com/pod-product-compliance
Ingram Content Group UK Ltd.
Pitfield, Milton Keynes, MK11 3LW, UK
UKHW040157230326
469255UK00012B/144